Will My Pet Go to Heaven?

Will My Pet Go to Heaven?

STEVE WOHLBERG

WINEPRESS WP PUBLISHING

Printed in the United States of America.

Packaged by WinePress Publishing, PO Box 428, Enumclaw, WA 98022. The views expressed or implied in this work do not necessarily reflect those of WinePress Publishing. The author is ultimately responsible for the design, content, and editorial accuracy of this work.

Cover Design: Gary Will, Texas Media Center.

ISBN 1-57921-485-1
Library of Congress Catalog Card Number: 2002107782

All things bright and beautiful,
All creatures great and small,
All things wise and wonderful,
The Lord God made them all.

—*Cecil F. Alexander* (1823–1895)

What dogs? These are my children, little people
with fur who make my heart open a little wider.

—*Oprah Winfrey* (b. 1954)

Dedicated to Fluffy
and all other friendly animals
through which God works to touch our hearts.

Table of Contents

Special Thanks

I didn't plan on writing this book. Its birth was unexpected. But so was the accident that took the life of our only pet—a tiny dog that had become like a person to us. That horrific moment, his last yelp, my wife's scream—these all seem forever etched in my brain. In the days that followed, as the thought of writing down our painful journey took more definite shape, my wife Kristin supported me all the way. Thank you, honey, for your love, encouragement, valuable suggestions, and editorial assistance.

I am grateful to our heavenly Father for creating such a wonderful world for us to live in—one that includes many funny, furry creatures who bring no small amount of happiness to our lives.

I also very much appreciate the kindness of God's Spirit who comforted our hearts after our loss—His presence that was clearly felt.

Above all, I want to thank the Crucified One, because it is through His awesome sacrifice that we will live forever with Him and *His animals* on the new earth.

Introduction

I care not for a man's religion whose dog and cat
are not the better for it.
Abraham Lincoln (1809–1865)

Believe it or not, millions of animal-loving human beings have
pondered at one time or another, *Will my pet go to heaven?* I
don't think this is an exaggeration because, first of all, this question often pops into The Question Box during my prophecy seminars. Secondly, a Christian woman who regularly gives home Bible
studies to people on various topics told me recently, "This is one
of *the* most common questions I get!"

Beyond this, based on the numerous pre-press comments I've
received from both friends and strangers, I realize that many are
extremely interested in my search for an answer to this question. A
tall redheaded woman once asked me, "When will your pet book
be finished? I know seven people who want to read it!" I talked to
a stranger at the Dallas airport in the line by the ticket counter; as
she clutched her own four-legged friend, she said earnestly, "I'll
buy it!"

Later that same day a man sat down beside me as we waited for
our rides from the Oklahoma City airport. With time to kill, I had

just booted up my computer laptop to work on this manuscript. "I'm writing a book," I commented, as we began a friendly visit. "About what?" he asked with interest. I told him, and before we parted, he said eagerly, "I'd like to read that book!" I could go on and on. Truly, this subject strikes a common chord in many hearts.

The reason is simple: *People really love their animals.*

The love for a horse is just as complicated as the love for another human being. . . . If you have never loved a horse, you will never understand.

—AUTHOR UNKNOWN

During this short life of ours it's easy to become attached to one of God's more intelligent, non-human creatures, be it a dog, a cat, a bird, a horse, or some other friendly companion. Dogs aren't called "Man's Best Friend" for nothing. For those that have them, pets truly become part of the family. They live, sleep, eat, play, cry, lick, cuddle, and prance around in and outside our homes. People build them their own little houses, buy them special treats, put funny clothes on them, take them on trips, check them into pet-friendly hotels, reserve spaces for them on airlines, watch them give birth to babies, take them to pet doctors when they're sick, pay big money for pet insurance, agonize as they go through major surgeries, and even include them in their wills and estate planning.

Many animals are quite smart, too. When they sense we're hurt, they do their furry best to bring comfort. In not a few cases, pets have both risked their lives or lost their lives in incredibly heroic efforts to save their owners. Dramatic tales involving these super-animals are often reported on the popular TV show, *Miracle Pets,* or on the *Animal Planet* channel. Some of these pets have even been awarded medals of honor.

Not surprisingly, when these almost-human companions breathe their last breaths, their deaths can cause the deepest pain. Many grief-strickened owners bury their animals under pet tombstones in pet cemeteries—cemeteries

Some of my best leading men have been dogs and horses.

—**ELIZABETH TAYLOR**

(b. 1932)

which are springing up around the world and offer a full line of cremation and burial services. After the heartbreaking funerals, animal graves are visited just like human graves. Pet photos are cherished just like pictures of parents, children, grandparents, brothers, and sisters. Many grieving humans turn to professional counselors who offer a variety of pet bereavement resources and support groups. And with the growth of twenty-first century techno-wizardry, more and more pet owners are considering the possibility of cloning their departed pet.

What should a parent say to a teary-eyed child who asks, after the family dog, cat, or horse dies, "Will Rover, Snow Ball, or Black Beauty be in heaven?" Answers like, "Of course, sweetheart," or, "Rover went to doggie heaven," are typical. But let's be serious. Are such responses simply fairy-tale talk that are as unreal as Santa Claus? Or is it possible that a heartbroken boy or girl (not to mention parent) may really see Rover, Snow Ball, or Black Beauty again?

This book is not about fairy tales, fiction, or fantasies like E.T., Star Wars, Jurassic Park, Lion King, or Shrek. Instead, it's about a heart-felt question, the Holy Bible, and the truth. Ever since I first began my spiritual quest, God has become very real to me, and He has proven His love many times. After studying the Bible for twenty-plus years, I'm totally convinced it is a Heaven-inspired book. In the midst of life's most painful struggles, aches, and pains, its soul-penetrating words and promises have brought real peace to my heart.

The Bible reveals a loving God who originally created a perfect Garden of Eden for both humans and animals. Without watering down reality, it describes the sin of Adam and Eve, its deadly effect on both man and beast, and also God's wonderful plan to restore Planet Earth to its original condition. Thankfully, if you peek at the final pages of the Bible, His love wins. A new earth is described in which will dwell both perfected people and many furry friends. The Good Book is very clear—both humans and animals will find a happy home in God's eternal kingdom. Read it for yourself:

> For behold, I create new heavens and a new earth; and the former shall not be remembered or come to mind . . . The wolf and the lamb shall feed together, The lion shall eat straw like the ox . . . They shall not hurt nor destroy in all My holy mountain, Says the Lord. (Isaiah 65:17,25)

In this book I will address the very real question asked by many aching hearts, "Will my pet go to heaven?" Yet from the get-go, just for the record, I must admit that no one knows with total, absolute certainty, except God Himself. So don't expect me to be super-*dog*matic (pun intended). And if there's a slight chance you are concerned about Steve Wohlberg drifting off into some kind of pet-heresy, don't worry, I won't. I have been very careful to maintain scriptural sanity, reasonableness, and common sense. I promise you, there's nothing extreme, weird, or bizarre in here.

In addition—now don't miss this point!—I didn't write *Will My Pet Go to Heaven?* to ignite any animal arguments or cat controversies. So please don't get into any *dog fights* over this topic; it's not worth it. After you have finished reading this book, I'm confident you'll see it as an insightful, friendly work; totally sensible, and 100% kosher. But more importantly, you'll be surprised to find that it reveals many unexpected, deep, and power-packed truths that may even change your life.

I'm about to open my heart to you, and to share an extremely traumatic and painful journey my wife Kristin and I passed through after the loss of a tiny friend. You will also learn my reasons—from the Bible no less—why we have come to embrace the hope of someday seeing our dog's happy face again. Above all, if your own heart is open, you are going to discover many surprising and wonderful insights into the character of our heavenly Friend. Here lies my ultimate reason for writing this book. I hope to direct the hearts of animal-loving human beings toward a truly magnificent and super-loving Creator who cares for us all.

I hope to see you in His eternal kingdom.

Dog Hero of the Year Awards

The average dog is a nicer person than the average person.
Andrew A. Rooney

Before I share my personal story of the tragic death of my much-loved pet, and of my subsequent investigation into the possibility of a heavenly reunion, I've chosen to introduce this book with two preliminary chapters which unquestionably reveal the intelligence, loyalty, and value of animals to humankind. Get ready for a pleasant thrill! In this first chapter, you're about to read a sequence of short, real-life news bites reporting incredible stories of super-pets which miraculously saved the lives of their owners. Then in chapter two, you'll learn about therapy dogs after September 11 at Ground Zero.

Since 1954, the world-famous producer of pet food—Heinz Pet Products—has granted an annual "Dog Hero of the Year" award to certain animals for noble feats of heroism. In fact, if it wasn't for the intensely purposeful, furry efforts of those wonderful, award-winning animals, many human beings would have died. After numerous submissions into the contest which described amazing life-and-death dramas, the following courageous canines finally won the prize:

Mehlville, Missouri, 1959: Lady, a mixed breed, frantically searched for help and brought back two telephone linemen to rescue a three-year-old boy who was sinking in a muddy swamp.

Euless, Texas, 1968: When his two-year-old master wandered away from home and started playing in the midst of traffic, Ringo the mixed breed barked and ran circles around the boy to divert oncoming cars.

John's Island, South Carolina, 1973: A 14-month-old Saint Bernard named Budweiser saved one of his owner's grandchildren, then another, by dragging them by their shirts from a burning house.

Cleveland, Ohio, 1980: Woodie, a mixed breed, broke his hip when he leaped from an eighty-foot cliff to rescue Ray, his owner's fiancé, who fell from the cliff and landed face down in a river. The wounded dog kept Ray's face above water until help arrived.

Dickenson, North Carolina, 1986: Together, Champ, a terrier, and Buddy, a mixed breed, led their owners to a nearby warehouse where an

It's character that counts. We should show unconditional love to our families, loyalty to our friends, and always seek to protect them from harm. When we fully attain such an exalted character, we will finally exhibit the normal traits of a dog.

—AUTHOR UNKNOWN

injured truck driver was trapped beneath a 2,680-pound earth mover tire.

Watsonville, California, 1989: During the San Francisco earthquake, Reona the Rottweiler saved a frightened five-year-old epileptic girl by pushing the child aside just before a microwave oven fell from the top of a refrigerator. The dog then calmed the young girl and prevented her from having a seizure.

Tullahoma, Tennessee, 1992: When Sparky's burly 227-pound owner, Bo, collapsed from a heart attack during a morning walk, this 130-pound yellow Labrador Retriever dragged his master nearly 200 yards. Bo made it to the hospital just in time for his condition to be stabilized.

Imperial Beach, California, 1993: During large scale flooding in Southern California's Tijuana River valley, Weela's repeated heroism over a three-month period saved 30 people, 29 dogs, 13 horses and one cat, all of whom otherwise may have perished in the flood.

Tucson, Arizona, 1996: Despite being shot five times by a home invader, Brandy kept up her fight and chased the attacker out, saving the life of his owner.

LaBelle, Florida, 2002: Two-year-old Blue, an Australian blue heeler, rescued his eighty-five-year-old owner from a vicious alligator attack and survived numerous injuries from the dangerous encounter.[1]

Therapy Dogs at Ground Zero

There is no psychiatrist in the world
like a puppy licking your face.
Ben Williams (1877–1964)

The week of September 11, 2001, has been appropriately labeled
". . . the week that changed America" (*Newsweek*, Sept. 24, p.
70).[2] On that fateful Tuesday morning, as I watched in horror the
unfolding news on our television screen, the second tower of the
World Trade Center collapsed right before my eyes. I will never forget it, at least not in this life.

Millions of us have seen—over and over again—the images on
CBS, NBC, and CNN of hijacked planes that became guided mis-
siles ramming into buildings, of doomed people jumping out of
flaming windows, and of noble fireman who risked their lives and
lost their lives trying to save others. Yet something else went almost unnoticed. As far as I know, it was not reported by Peter
Jennings on ABC World News Tonight, or by any other news anchor. Nevertheless, it was real—and extremely important—to those
whose lives were touched. It was the story of the incredible comfort that paws, whiskers, and animal tongues brought to human
beings at Ground Zero.

The following paragraphs, article, and poem were taken from www.tdi-dog.org, the official internet home page of *Therapy Dogs International, Inc.* Founded in 1976, TDI has for many years trained and sent animals to bring warmth, love, and healing to people in need. After September 11, TDI workers and volunteers—along with their dogs—came to New York to help.

The use of canines to help mankind is known throughout the world. They have been used for guarding flocks, tracking, hunting, search and rescue, leading the blind, and in assisting the deaf and physically challenged. The bond between dog and man dates back to early history, but it wasn't until recently that a correlation was acknowledged between this bond and the emotional

I love a dog. He does nothing for political reasons.
—**WILL ROGERS** (1879–1935)

health of humans. Studies have shown that a person holding or petting an animal will cause a lowering of blood pressure, the release of strain and tension, and can draw out a person from loneliness and depression.[3]

Professional Therapist Witnesses TDI Relief in NYC

As a therapist, I have used dogs in my work for over twenty years. I firmly believe that animals have a profoundly positive impact on our physical and emotional health and well being. I watch as my dogs turn that belief into reality each and every day.

Following the tragic events of September 11, 2001, I received a call from TDI to volunteer at the Family Assistance Center on

Pier 94 in NYC. Despite my many years of using my dogs to help soothe and calm others, this would be my biggest crisis intervention experience ever. It was an honor to able to help in this most magical and rewarding way.

A quote by Allen Schoen and Pam Proctor has been a guiding principle for me in my work. In their book entitled, *Love, Miracles, and Animal Healing,* they state, "By their very presence in our midst, animals awaken in us the desire to respond and to love." The work that our Therapy Dogs accomplished in NYC really exemplified this and it brought to the forefront the profound and compelling bond between humans and animals. As our dogs were approached by each and every person, they instantly responded with compassion and love—no questions, no tough demands. Their touch brought warmth and comfort to many broken hearts. They helped people to relax—perhaps even to open up a bit and let the words—or the tears—begin. For others, the dogs brought a smile to their faces—a brief but important respite from the shocking pain and sorrow. For the children, they brought joy and comfort—a safe bridge between child and adult—a way to connect, a chance amidst the confusion and sadness to laugh and to play. For the other volunteers and relief workers, our dogs were invaluable in providing a break from the intensity of emotion. They brought a sense of normalcy to these abnormal times,

> One reason the dog has so many friends: He wags his tail instead of his tongue.
>
>  **—AUTHOR UNKNOWN**

a simplicity amidst the chaos, and they created a cozy sense of security and warmth throughout the Center.

In short, our dogs have played a valuable role in helping others to begin the healing process after the tragedy of September 11. They have also helped all of us to put things in perspective and to reconnect with life's simple and most important values. It never ceases to amaze me how quickly and effectively our dogs can touch others' hearts and help them to heal. Despite my years of training, experience, and education, I will always believe that sometimes the most effective kind of therapy begins with a cold, wet nose and ends with the wag of a tail. I know that in NYC, there are many that would agree.

—Nanette Winter, M.A. Director of Psychological Services, Northstar Industries, Saranac Lake, NY; TDI Evaluator[4]

Sarah Sypniewski, a 23-year-old caseworker for the Red Cross, was also assigned to work at the Family Assistance Center at Pier 94 in New York City just a few weeks after the World Trade Center collapsed. Her task was to evaluate the victims who came to the center, and to give general guidance as to where they might receive assistance in those days of crisis. Day by day, as those with needs came to her for help, she had a hard time holding herself together, much less helping others. Yet as a result of TDI's therapy dogs—who showed up every day at the pier—she was able to make it through. Daily the dogs approached both workers and victims, bringing a sense of hope, relief, and friendliness into an otherwise almost unbearable situation.

On the day before she left New York for her return flight to California, she penned this memorable poem to honor the gentle animals that had so deeply soothed her soul:

Paws Amidst Pain

Dedicated to the therapy dogs at PIER 94 in NYC
who worked so hard responding to the human mess of 9/11,
particularly to my special friend, Wusel.
Thank you, dogs and humans, for your undying love.

The hours upon hours you pad through these paths of pain,
are the hours you help us see the light through the pouring rain.
You never falter, never fail, and always call to mind,
the joy and inspiration that's sometimes hard to find.
As we muddle through the wreckage that's half hope and half despair,
You stand by like an anchor, tail wagging in the air.

With every touch you heal us, from fur to human heart,
solace in each stroke, you prevent our falling apart.
You never complain and though you cry, you do not show your tears,
you swallow them back, hold your post, and calm so many fears.
Your spirit penetrates our beings right into our souls,
you let us touch and talk to you as we try to fill the holes.

There are times we want to just give up and head back to our homes,
and there you are with pricked up ears, and then we're not alone.
You sigh, surrender, and knowingly roll onto your back;
"Here's my tummy—you can have it . . . just give me a snack."

Will My Pet Go to Heaven?

You do so much for us we just can't do ourselves,
you specialize in soulspeak that never ceases to delve
straight into the place we do not talk about.
You let us cry and let us laugh and get all of it out.

So before I go, I want to say I hope you know the truth:
You saved me every single day,
I survived because of you.[5]

by Sarah Sypniewski
L.A. County Program Coordinator
National Readiness and Response Corps
Written on 11/02/01

3

Our Dog's Name Was Jax

I once had a sparrow alight upon my shoulder for a moment,
while I was hoeing in a village garden, and I felt that I was more
distinguished by that circumstance that I should have been by
any epaulet I could have worn.

Henry David Thoreau (1817–1862)

Will Steve Wohlberg ever get married?" my closest friends
had wondered for years. Even my parents were starting to
doubt. But finally, at the ripe age of 41, I shocked them all by saying, "I do," in the presence of hundreds of guests inside a large
church in California. Neither Kristin—formerly Kristin Renee
Demarest—nor I had ever been married before, and this was the
very special beginning of our new life together. The hit song, "You've
Only Just Begun," applied perfectly. For years I had lived alone in
tiny apartments, but now it was time for a house. In January of
2000, a few days after the much-feared Y2K glitch became the new
millennium's most famous fizzle, I purchased a house for my new
bride in a rather cozy residential section in Fort Worth, Texas. This
was our first home.

It took me forty-one years to get married, and at this point I
wasn't quite ready for any little Wohlbergs running around, so we
decided to get a dog. Kristin liked the idea of a little one, and soon
we found Jax. His original owners, Mark and Cortney Cooper, lived

in the country just outside of Fort Worth. Because we are all very close friends, my wife and I often visit their home, sometimes even staying over on weekends. As a result of a certain circumstance, their little Jax needed a new home. One day, as the four of us talked about how Kristin and I were on the lookout for a pet, and they were searching for new owners, the fit seemed perfect. So Jax became our first dog.

> Dogs come when they're called; cats take a message and get back to you later.
>
> —MARY BLY

Officially, Jax was a toy rat terrier, although we never cared much for the "rat" part. These "toy" dogs are quite small, and even when fully grown, they're not normally more than 6–8 lbs. In addition, Jax was a runt, which means he was the smallest of his litter. He was about two years old when we placed him in my Ford Explorer to come home with us.

When we took him in, Jax wasn't sure if we were friends or foes. As a two-year old in a strange house with new "parents," he panicked just a bit. During our first absence, we later discovered he had scratched up the windowsill near a rear door in the sunroom trying to get out. Maybe he wasn't sure if we were coming back or not. He did this for three or four days each time we left. Yet Jax was a highly intelligent little guy. Each time we went away, he soon realized we did come back. After a few days of nurture, love, and a few fanny-whacks, he quickly settled down and became almost the perfect dog.

When Kristin or I drove up to our house, Jax was often watching for us from the bay window near the front door. As we walked in, he would dance around in circles in the funniest way! He always wanted to be with us. In whatever room we entered, he was there. One time Kristin went into her clothes closet just for a minute, left, and closed the door. Later she walked back in and found Jax! Often as I sat in front of my computer he would gently kick me with his paw as if to say, "Please let me up!" At night we would pick him up and plop him on our bed. As Kristin and I prayed

> The sound of birds stops the noise in my mind.
> —**CARLY SIMON** (b. 1945)

together, we would often add, ". . . and Lord, thank you also for our little Jax!" When the lights went out, our furry friend would slip under the covers and snuggle up close.

During the months that followed our attachment for Jax deepened. I often thought, *What a great dog!* He was so cute-looking that when we took him out for walks on his little leash to a small lake near our home, cars would sometimes slow down and those inside would point as if to say, "Look at that little fella!" Everyone liked him. He was friendly to our guests, played with their kids, and would sometimes just race around the house in a big circle just because he was happy. He had his favorite little rope which he would often grab and shake like a toy. He became so much a part of our family that Kristin's mother once called and asked, "How's my grand-dog?" Our home is a Christian home—which included me, Kristin, Jesus, and of course, Jax.

Those were wonderful days.

The Day Tragedy Struck

4

Until one has loved an animal,
a part of one's soul remains unawakened.
Anatole France (1844–1924)

Jax lived with us for almost a year. One Saturday evening, on October 27, 2001, the three of us drove out to visit with Mark, Cortney, and a group of other friends at their home in the country. The event was called, "The Fall Festival." It was a night of pleasant interaction, bonfires, and hayrides. We stayed the night, and, of course, Jax slept with us. On Sunday morning, our "little boy" stuck to us like glue, not wanting to get left behind. In retrospect, I wish we had left him. In any event, at about 2:00 P.M., we headed south towards our home in Fort Worth. As usual, Jax sat on Kristin's lap and licked the window for most of the trip. That was the last happy car ride he would ever take.

I parked the Explorer right in front of our home, along side the curb, facing east. As I got out, Jax jumped out with me. As I walked to the back of the vehicle to get our bags, Jax skipped around with me and then onto our grassy lawn towards our front door. As I reached for our things, I glanced to my right and saw him happily prancing around near my wife. At that very moment my heart felt such joy. I remember this distinctly. *I sure love that dog!* were my exact thoughts. As I turned back to the car to grab our bags, it was right then that tragedy struck!

I'll never forget it, at least not in this life. I didn't see it coming, but another SUV rounded the corner in front of me and drove right past me on my left side just a few feet from our car. "Jax!" Kristin screamed. I immediately turned to my left and saw his little yapping form dart underneath the other car. In a split-second of sheer horror I saw my tiny friend moving to bite the large left rear tire from underneath. I think he was trying to protect me, but he was no match for such a gigantic machine. As his tiny teeth bit the wheel near its front, the force of its forward-circular-downward motion quickly rammed his little head brutally into the ground. The car drove on, its driver never even knowing what had happened. So there Jax lay, motionless on the hot concrete, as if dead.

It may sound unbelievable, but in my 42 years of living, I have hardly ever felt such pain! "He's gone!" I yelled to my wife. As the tears gushed out, I had to look away. Just then another car came from the opposite direction right toward Jax as he lay bleeding in

> The mother eagle teaches her little ones to fly by making their nest so uncomfortable that they are forced to leave it and commit themselves to the unknown world of air outside. And just so does our God to us. He stirs up our comfortable nests, and pushes us over the edge of them, and we are forced to use our wings to save ourselves from fatal falling. Read your trials in this light, and see if you cannot begin to get a glimpse of their meaning. Your wings are being developed.
> **—HANNAH WHITHALL SMITH**
> (1832–1911)

the middle of the street. I bolted out in front of the car, waved both of my arms frantically, and shouted wildly, "No! . . . Please! . . . Stop!" The lady stopped, and after saying, "I'm so, so sorry!" she drove carefully around two sobbing "parents."

It was an absolute nightmare. In the midst of the street, I knelt in front of our dog and moaned loudly, "Oh, Jax! Why did you do that? Why? Why? Why!" I was devastated. Then all of a sudden Kristin cried out, "Steve, he's moving!" My first thought was, *How horrible! Now I'll have to kill him so he won't suffer.* "Let's take him to the Vet!" Kristin yelled. With a sense of utter hopelessness, I complied. I ran into the house, grabbed a towel, rushed back outside, and sadly wrapped Jax up. As we got into the car, I placed him on Kristin's lap. Then we raced away.

On the way to the Vet, Jax started writhing and wiggling. "He's in his death struggle! You take him!" Kristin pleaded. So we switched places and she drove. We went to two animal hospitals, but no one was there on a Sunday. Fortunately, at our third try we found Dr. Morris and his wife doing some clean-up work at the Southwestern Animal Clinic of Fort Worth. By this time Jax was really squirming around, yet obviously without consciousness. The side of his face was bleeding, his neck seemed out of whack, and his eyes showed no sign of seeing anything. "I'll need to run some tests," Dr. Morris said after giving Jax a sedative. "Go home. I'll call you in a couple of hours."

In my heart, somewhere, a flicker of hope sprang up.

5

From Sunday to Wednesday

My little dog—a heartbeat at my feet.
Edith Wharton (1862–1937)

The phone rang at about 5:30 that same Sunday afternoon. I was almost afraid to answer it. *Is Jax dead?* I wondered. "This is Dr. Morris. We've X-rayed his entire body and he has no broken bones or fractures. But he definitely has a concussion and his tiny brain is swollen. I'll call you again at about 9:00 tonight. That's it for now. Goodbye."

When I heard those words, everything in me knew it was time for prayer. "God, I know he's just a little dog, but, he's all we have. We have grown to love him so much! You made him, so *please, please,* save his life!" The next three days were quite amazing. This may sound silly, but we started a prayer chain for our little dog.

On Monday morning I was back at the Vet's and by this time I was starting to feel like a father visiting his sick child in the hospital! Our little dog had improved slightly, although not significantly. Mostly, he just lay on the table, twitching and jerking. By Tuesday, though, he was calmer, and even able to hold his head up. "He sometimes lifts his head and seems to look at me as I walk by his cage," the nurse remarked. "Once I even saw him twirling around on his front legs, trying to walk."

Come on Jax, you can make it! I thought. Yet his eyes showed little responsiveness.

"We hope that in a few days, after the swelling goes down in his brain, his mind will come back," she explained.

"Is it OK if I say a prayer in here?"

"Sure," the lady replied. So, I drew close to his little ear and breathed out a few words to God. Amazingly, immediately after my prayer, Jax lifted his little head, turned, and looked right at me!

> An animal's eyes have the power to speak a great language.
> —**MARTIN BUBER** (1878–1965)

On Tuesday he remained stable, with additional slight improvements. After counseling with Dr. Morris, Kristin and I decided that on Wednesday afternoon we would take him home in hopes that, through being with us once again, he might muster his dwindling life forces and stage a super-Jax-comeback. After all, he was a tough little dog! Because he wasn't able to eat by himself, his nurses were feeding him intravenously. "He'll be fed, hydrated, and ready when you come back tomorrow."

Sadly, I drove home.

6

Halloween: Night of Death

There was a handsome male mockingbird that sang his heart out every morning during the nesting season from the top of a tall Norfolk pine tree. Last week the tree was cut down. The mockingbird and his song are gone. I can't put a dollar value on the tree nor on the mockingbird nor on his song. But I know that I—and our whole neighborhood—have suffered a loss.
I wouldn't know how to count it in dollars.
Jacquelyn Hiller

With a tightening knot in my stomach, Kristin and I drove back to the clinic on Wednesday afternoon at about 4:30. When the nurse brought Jax out and placed him in my arms, not much had changed. He was still stable though, a bit thinner, with one really glassy eye. Our plan was to take him home and then, after an hour or so, to have Mark and Cortney join us. By surrounding Jax with quadruple love, we all hoped he might revive.

We pulled up in front of our house, the scene of the accident. Walking past the exact spot where his head hit the ground three days earlier, I slowly and gently carried Jax in my arms through the front door. "You're back, Jax! Smell your doggie food, isn't it familiar? Here's our bedroom, remember? Now we're in your favorite room—the sunroom! See that squirrel outside the window?

You always liked to bark at it. Jax, can you hear us? Jax! We love you!" No response. It was heartbreaking.

I laid him gently on a blanket on the floor near the center of the sunroom, and soon Mark and Cortney arrived. Then something astonishing happened. As the four

We call them dumb animals, and so they are, for they cannot tell us how they feel, but they do not suffer less because they have no words.

 —ANNA SEWELL,
Author of *Black Beauty* (1820–1878)

of us gathered close around his tiny doggie body, Jax distinctly moaned once, then again. "He knows we're here," Mark said. "He wants to respond, but he can't. He's in pain."

Before I left to go to our Wednesday night prayer meeting, we all knelt sadly beside our dog's motionless head. "Dear God, we love Jax so much, and we know You love him, too. Please, if it's Your will, heal him. If not, let him rest in peace. Oh God, give us a sign, one way or another, so we'll know what to do! We place his frail life in Your hands. In Jesus' name we pray, Amen." The reason I asked for a sign is because we didn't know how long we should try to maintain his existence if he didn't recover. Jax hadn't left us a will with instructions on when to pull the plug. Then I left for church.

Leading out in prayer meeting was very difficult that night. My heart ached, and my legs were weak. I finally told the group what was happening, and the name "Jax" was added to our prayer list. After my closing remarks a lady said to me, "I know of a German

Shepherd who was hit on the head by an on-coming train. He was knocked out for weeks, but he recovered! Don't give up hope!" I hadn't, and I was soon heading back to Kristin, Mark, and Cortney.

When I walked into our house I discovered they had moved Jax out of the sunroom into the living room. "His legs were getting cold," Kristin said quietly. It was about 9:00 P.M. We all sat around the living room and talked for a while. Then I went over to Jax and felt his legs. "He's getting colder," I said softly as I grabbed a few more blankets. His breathing also seemed quieter. Something was happening, I could feel it. His little body was closing down. "I think he's dying," I whispered.

> Hear and bless Thy beasts and singing birds, and guard with tenderness, small things that have no words.
>
> **—AUTHOR UNKNOWN**

The Nightly News came on at 10:00 P.M. Terrorism and Anthrax were the top stories. Then the usual stock market report. I don't remember if the NASDAQ went up or down. After that, some local news. It was Halloween evening, and the reports were positive. All was quiet, with no major events in Fort Worth. A few kids had come by and knocked on our door, but we were hardly in the mood to even answer. Kristin had planned to give out little boxes of raisins that night, but she forgot to buy them at a market down the street.

When the Nightly News was over, at about 10:30 P.M., I rose from the couch and walked over to Jax. He was laying by the fireplace, completely still. His eyes were still open. I pulled off the blankets, and slowly reached for his fast-cooling body. Nothing. No movement at all. I shook him slightly. Still nothing. Mark moved over and felt near his heart. "He's dead." I then picked Jax up and held his face close to mine. I even lit a match and held it near his little mouth. No flicker. "Yes. He's gone." We cried, and accepted this as God's will. Then I kissed my tiny friend for the last time.

As I look back on the events of that night, it all seems so amazing. Jax had been stable for three days. When we brought him home, his distinct moan told us he knew we were there. It was as if he wanted so badly to say, "Yes! I hear you! I love you, too! I'm trying to respond, but I can't!" It was like he was trapped inside a broken brain. We had prayed, and even asked for a sign, then we trusted our "little boy" to our Father's heart.

The mystery of love is greater than the mystery of death.

—AUTHOR UNKNOWN

In retrospect, I really think Jax made a decision to die. Maybe this was the only way he could respond to us. He was finally home in our house, away from the strange clinic, and he knew it. The four human beings who loved him the most were there by his side. After our prayer, within a very short time, his body shut down, and that was it. We rapped his small lifeless form in a blanket, put it in a box, and placed it in our cold garage.

Mark and Cortney decided to stay the night. In the morning I sadly placed the box in their pickup truck, and they took him out to their country property to bury him. That's where Jax grew up. His tiny grave is still there today.

My Personal Search Begins

7

I was gratified to be able to answer promptly.
I said, "I don't know."
Mark Twain (1835–1910)

he next day after Jax died, I sadly sat down at my Hewlett-Packard desktop computer to send out some e-mail to a few friends who I knew had been praying for our dog. After opening up Microsoft Outlook, I brought up the first letter. With great difficulty I typed into the subject line, J A X   I S   D E A D. It was awful. At this point, I didn't have the slightest thought about ever seeing him again, and certainly not about writing this book! Yes, people had asked me before, "Steve, do you think our pets might be in heaven?" but I hadn't taken the question very seriously. After sending the first e-mail, I did the usual copy-and-paste thing. One by one, I clicked "send."

Within a short time, a good friend from Canada responded with a rather unexpected note. He basically said, "After Jesus Christ comes, you'll see Jax again in a new doggie body!" *What a nice thought,* I mused. But still, I didn't take it seriously. Why should I? The central focus of the Bible is God, people, and human salvation, not dogs and cats, right?

Then a second friend from Alaska who had been praying for Jax e-mailed me back. This young man has a wife, two children, and two cats. Unknown to me, he was a great animal lover. In an attempt to give comfort, he not only expressed his personal hope that we might someday see our pets again, but then he gave this reason: He said our loving God just might bring them back to life again as a gift for those who are saved. Somehow, the five little words—*for those who are saved*—really affected me. Mysteriously, they struck a new note inside my soul.

For the next few moments I just sat there stunned, staring silently at my computer monitor. *Could it be?* Suddenly, something deep inside my heart seemed to change. Part of the pain was lifted.

I sensed a very definite and loving presence draw near. I have felt this presence many times throughout the course of my spiritual journey, but never in this context.

A wise old owl sat in an oak,
The more he saw the less he spoke,
The less he spoke the more he heard,
Now wasn't he a wise old bird?

—AUTHOR UNKNOWN

Just then, an unexpected feeling of hope sprang up! "It's time for some research into a new topic!" I told myself.

God Loves Animals, Too!

Not even a sparrow, worth only half a penny, can fall to the
ground without your Father knowing it.
Jesus Christ (Matthew 10:29 NLT)

In the last few years, I have written a number of fast-selling books and have traveled extensively speaking on Bible topics, especially the mysterious prophecies of the book of Revelation. My ministry has also taken me into the arena of radio and international television. I think it's safe to say that among my readers, listeners, and viewers, I've developed a reputation for presenting credible and well-researched information. But after Jax died, I entered an entirely new field of study. I wanted to see what the Bible might have to say about animals!

I was amazed at what I found. Going back to Genesis (the Bible's very first book), I carefully re-examined the creation account. Chapter one describes how God made everything by simply speaking. Then chapter two becomes more personal as Moses related how "the Lord God formed man from the dust of the earth" (v. 7). This showed me God's special interest in man. OK, but what about the animals?

Then I read, "Out of the ground the Lord God formed every beast of the field . . ." (v. 19). This taught me that God not only carefully crafted man out of the earth, but also that He made the animals from the same chunk of ground. It's true, only man was created in the image of God (1:26), yet the animals were also purposefully and specifically "formed" by Him. I was impressed with a number of things. First, the very idea of "animals" came from God Himself. He conceived of, designed, built, and then brought them to life. Second, all animals are therefore primarily *God's animals,* for He made them. Third, He cares for them, or else why spend heavenly time and divine energy forming them at all?

> But now ask the beasts, and they will teach you;
> And the birds of the air, and they will tell you;
> Or speak to the earth, and it will teach you;
> And the fish of the sea will explain to you.
> Who among all these does not know
> That the hand of the Lord has done this,
> In whose hand is the life of every living thing,
> And the breath of all mankind?
>
> **—JOB 12:7–10**

"Out of the ground the Lord God formed every beast of the field and every bird of the air, and brought them to Adam to see what he would call them. And whatever Adam called each living creature, that was its name. So Adam gave names to all cattle, to the birds of the air, and to every beast of the field" (2:19, 20). This was even more interesting! A light went on in my head. I realized that in the Bible, which is the most important book ever written, one of the very first assignments God gave to man after He formed him was to name animals!

Just think of it! How exciting it must have been for Adam to suddenly find himself surrounded by an entire group of fuzzy, furry, woolly, feathery, purring, yapping, cooing, chirping, happy creatures! Then I thought, *Why did God make these creatures in the first place?* Upon further reflection, the answer seemed rather simple.

Originally, God didn't make His creatures to be killed and processed into McDonald's hamburgers or Kentucky Fried Chicken. Not at all. This only came later, and is the result of man's sin. Instead, the Lord made them because He is an intensely creative, highly personal, and extremely loving God (1 John 4:8) who simply wanted to enhance Adam's happiness and enjoyment. In other words, the animals were initially created by God to be man's friends, not his food: his pets, not his pork chops. So the Lord made them, and brought them to Adam. I imagine He said something like, "Here's some new friends! Now give them names." Later Eve came along, but that's another story.

When Adam and Eve sinned in Genesis 3, God's original plan was shattered and His whole creation was affected. Thankfully, His love for human beings didn't change one bit. But what about the animals? Does the Lord still care for them, even after the fall? In the midst of my is-there-hope-for-Jax research, I soon turned to the small book of Jonah. As I leafed through the pages, three words stuck out. Before I hardly noticed them, but now they practically jumped off the page!

At the very end of this most unusual story, Jonah became upset because God decided not to punish the wicked, party-crazed city of Nineveh after all because its inhabitants had responded to His warning. In a merciful response to His unreasonable prophet, the Lord inquired, "Should I not pity Nineveh, that great city, in which are more than one hundred and twenty thousand persons who cannot discern between their right hand and their left—*and much livestock?*" (Jonah 4:11, italics added).

How marvelous! God not only pitied those sin-loving, disoriented humans in the city of Nineveh, but He also felt compassion for the mooing cows, baaing sheep, and bleating goats! These three words, "and much livestock," revealed to me God's tender love and compassion for even the animals that lived there. Think about it. If He cared back then, don't you think He still pities the pets in New York, Los Angeles, Russia, Afghanistan, and all over the world? Of course He does, for the Good Book says He is "the same yesterday, today, and forever" (Hebrews 13:8).

> O Lord, You preserve both man and beast.
> —**PSALM 36:6**

As my research continued, I discovered another Bible story that really touched my heart. As with the book of Jonah, I'd read it before, but now I was ripe for another fresh insight from our heavenly Friend. It was the story of a-prophet-gone-bad named Balaam who abused his faithful donkey. As the two of them trotted down an isolated and dusty road, a holy angel with an unsheathed sword suddenly stood before them both, yet only the donkey saw him. Three times the donkey veered off the path to save his master's life. Finding his animal's actions totally unexplainable, Balaam cruelly reacted three times with a kick and a fist.

We can judge the heart of a man by his treatment of animals.

—IMMANUEL KANT

(1724–1804)

Finally the angel became visible to the eyes of the astonished prophet. "The Angel of the Lord said to Balaam, 'Why have you struck your donkey these three times?'" (Numbers 22:32). Here we see a heavenly angel visiting earth and rebuking a human for his unreasonable harshness toward his four-legged friend! Besides this, after complimenting the heroic efforts of the donkey, the angel said to Balaam, "If she had not turned aside from me, surely I would also have killed you by now, *and let her live*" (v. 33, italics added). As a writer who likes to use his imagination, I could almost picture this headline, "Heavenly Being Kills Man but Saves Animal Alive." As with Genesis and the story of Jonah, another "click" occurred inside my mental computer. Not only does God love animals, *but so do His angels.*

I soon discovered that even the Ten Commandments reveal God's care for animals. The fourth commandment says,

> Remember the Sabbath day, to keep it holy. Six days you shall labor and do all your work, but the seventh day is the Sabbath of the Lord your God, in it you shall do no work: you, nor your son, nor your daughter, nor your male servant, nor your female servant, *nor your cattle,* nor your stranger who is within your gates. For in six days the Lord made the heavens and the earth, the sea, and all that is in them, and rested on the seventh day. Therefore the Lord blessed the Sabbath day, and hallowed it. (Exodus 20:8-11, italics added)

The fourth commandment reveals God as the all-powerful Creator of heaven and earth. After making Planet Earth in six literal, 24-hour days, God rested on the seventh day. His law commands us to cease from secular work on the Sabbath so we can focus on our Maker, meditate on His creative power revealed in nature, and above all, get to know Him better. Yet it's not only people who are to rest. If you look closely, God's love extends even to the mooing cows, for they also are to take a break from plowing the fields (v. 10).

The Bible says the Ten Commandments were "written with the finger of God" on two tables of stone (Exodus 31:18). This shows the permanent nature of this law. Therefore the words, "nor your cattle" (v. 10), being indelibly carved into solid rock by God Himself, demonstrate the Almighty's permanent interest in animals. Yet there's more. If you think about it, that tiny and often overlooked phrase, "nor your cattle," being part of God's moral law, also raises the issue of man's treatment of animals to a moral level. "Nor your cattle" ultimately means that human beings have a certain moral obligation to care for the needs of God's animals, and to treat them kindly.

A righteous man regards the life of his animal.

—PROVERBS 12 :10

The biblical truth about our Creator is of mega-importance. It also contains hidden depths. The Bible's last and most mysterious book—"The Revelation"—reveals a special end-time message emphasizing this very truth. It is to be communicated "to every nation, tribe, tongue and people" before the second coming of Jesus Christ (Revelation 14:6, 14-16). This high-impact, life and death message proclaims, "Worship Him who *made* heaven and earth, the sea and springs of water" (v. 7, italics added).

Let's go deeper. Who specifically is the One who made heaven and earth—that is, the Milky Way, earth's continents, the Pacific Ocean, the Nile River, the animals in the San Diego Zoo, and everything else in existence? A careful study of the New Testament reveals it was actually Jesus Christ, who is "equal with God" (Philippians 2:6). The Bible says that our heavenly Father "created all things *through* Jesus Christ" (Ephesians 3:9, italics added).

Notice carefully: "He [Jesus Christ] was in the world, and *the world was made by Him,* and the world knew Him not" (John 1:10, KJV, italics added). Did you catch that? The power-packed message of this simple verse is that the Bethlehem Baby was really the Creator Himself coming to earth in the form of a human being. So what does this mean to us animal lovers? Simply this: It means that every dog, cat, bird, horse, dolphin—or any other creature—was actually thoughtfully designed, purposefully planned, and uniquely created by the very same One who ultimately gave His life on a splintery cross! In other words, all animals are *really Jesus Christ's animals*. He made them, He loves them, and they're His pets, too.

A horse is an angel without wings.
—AUTHOR UNKNOWN

The Lord says,

> For every beast of the forest *is Mine,* and the cattle on a thousand hills. I know all the birds of the mountains, And the wild beasts of the field *are Mine.* (Psalm 50:10,11 italics added)

"The Lord is good to all, and His tender mercies are over all His works" (Psalm 145:9). Our Lord has "tender" thoughts toward "all" His works, which certainly would include His animals. Now ask yourself this question: Whenever a human being's beloved dog, cat, bird, or horse gets hit by a car, drowns, dies from some disease, or simply wastes away from old age, does their Maker feel no pain? Their earthly owners do. Why is this? The answer is simple, yet profound. The reason is because human beings were made in the image of God, and the Lord suffers, too. If we who are in God's image feel such grief over the loss of an animal we have grown to love, then surely our pain must reveal a unique window into His heavenly heart.

I was really shocked to discover the depths of feeling that pulsated through my own aching heart when our tiny rat terrier died. In the days that followed, Kristin and I suffered a lot. It was hard to see that certain brown pillow on the couch in our living room on which Jax loved to sit. It brought tears to my eyes to see his little bowl still filled with Jax-food in the kitchen. And then there was that little Jax-photo of his doggie face on our dresser in the master bedroom. For many days, as we walked around the house, we imagined him everywhere! Everything seemed so unreal. Was he really gone, or was this a bad dream? Then I thought, *Where do such feelings come from anyway?* As hard as it was, I learned a mega-lesson about God's love through my grief. The lesson was: He cares more than we realize—even for Jax.

Before I close this chapter I want to share one more precious insight about God's love, not for animals, but for people. Look carefully at these words: "For the invisible things of him from the creation of the world are clearly seen, being understood by the things that are made" (Romans 1:20, KJV). Get it? Paul said we understand "the invisible things" of God's character by looking at "the things that are made." In other words, God reveals aspects of His personality to us through His created works. That's why, in addition to the Bible, nature is called His second book.

God "made" Jax, right? When he was alive, every time I came home—and I mean *every time*—he could hardly wait to jump and start licking me! In my minds-eye I can still see his stubby tail wiggling. The more I think about it, our dog's love was ever-constant, even after those rare occasions when I had to spank his terrier-fanny for pooping or peeing on the carpet. No matter what, his love remained. Truly, Jax was a super-affectionate dog.

After his death I thought about his doggie-love more distinctly. *Where did such love come from anyway?* Surely, it came from God. Our Creator made his wiggling tail, licking tongue, and loving heart. Why did He make these things in the first place? There can be only one answer. The reason is because God's "invisible" heart must be filled with wonderful love, and He must have chosen to reveal a portion of that love through His animals. Maybe that's why Job wrote so long ago, "But now ask the beasts, and they will teach you" (Job 12:7).

Therefore when any friendly creature of God—be it a dog, a cat, a bird, or a horse—prances, purrs, chirps, yaps, licks, snuggles, or tries to love us in any way, something fantastic is happening. We may not understand it, and it may roll right past us like the proverbial water off a duck's back, but we are witnessing a tiny glimpse of a super-creative and all-wise Creator's personal love for us through one of His love letters.

A meow massages the heart.

—STUART MCMILLAN

So, the next time your horse gently nudges you, or your cat snuggles up against you, or a little puppy licks you, or your fully-grown faithful friend barks to protect you from danger, just think about this: Someone in heaven may be trying to say, "I love you," through your pet.

9

Will My Pet Go to Heaven?

I never meant you to be
Dog of My Heart,
But without speech you spoke to me,
Without hands you touched me,
Without reproach you humbled me.
And while I know there would have never been
A long-enough life, or the right time to say good-bye,
I will wait, however long it takes,
To get beyond my miserable state of grief and pain,
Towards warm and comforting
Remembrance,
And gratitude,
For the joy you brought me,
For the truths you taught me.

I never meant you to be
Dog of My Heart,
I only meant for you to mean as much.
But you meant
So much more.

Lillian Sugahara (b. 1955)

Is there any hope for Jax?" I asked myself seriously. I know, he was just a dog, but Kristin and I had come to love that tiny ball of fur. Now that I had definite proof from the Bible that God not only created and loves His animals, but even reveals a portion of His own love through them, I decided to look for other passages that might reveal the possibility—however remote—that we might someday see our little dancing, funny friend again.

In this chapter I am going to share with you the results of my search and journey. As I said before, I can't say for sure whether our pets will be in heaven. Ultimately, that's up to God. The Bible doesn't say in black and white, "Your dog, cat, or horse will some-day have wings." Nevertheless, I have found some very significant passages which I think do suggest *the strong possibility* that at least some of this world's sin-suffering animals might transition over to "the other side." Of course, you must come to your own conclusion.

First, the Bible does plainly teach that a new world is coming. The very last Bible writer, whose name was John, declared, "I saw a new heaven and a new earth, for the first heaven and the first earth had passed away . . . And God will wipe away every tear from their eyes; there shall be no more death, nor sorrow, nor crying. There shall be no more pain, for the former things have passed away" (Rev. 21:1, 4). Peter also wrote, "Nevertheless we, accord-ing to His promise, look for new heavens and a new earth in which righteousness dwells" (2 Peter 3:13).

In that happy place there'll be no more terrorist-hijackers, sui-cide-bombers, heart-disease, arthritis, pain, smog, or taxes to pay to the IRS. We also have the assurance that animals will be there, too. The Good Book says, "The wolf also shall dwell with the lamb, the leopard shall lie down with the young goat, the calf and the young lion and the fatling together; And a little child shall lead them . . . They shall not hurt nor destroy in all My holy mountain, For the earth shall be full of the knowledge of the glory of the Lord as the waters cover the sea" (Isaiah 11:6, 9).

Therefore, according to 2 Peter 3 and Isaiah 11, not only will saved human beings be there, but so will wolves, lions, leopards, goats, and probably lots of other animals. In that wonderful place, wolves won't snarl, lions won't bite, and leopards won't be scary. God's promise is, "They shall not hurt nor destroy in all My holy mountain." Won't that be great?

It seems to me that when it comes to those future kingdom-creatures, God has three options:

Option #1: He can create entirely new animals from scratch.
Option #2: He can bring back to life animals that have suffered in our present world, giving them immortal bodies.
Option #3: He can make some new animals and bring back some old ones as well.

Unless there is some unrevealed factor preventing Him from doing so, I think the all-powerful God can accomplish any or all of these options. His Word says, "Behold, I am the Lord, the God of all flesh. Is there anything too hard for Me?" (Jeremiah 32:27). If God wants to re-create in the new world some of the animals from this old world, it's an easy task. Besides, by then He will have already accomplished something much more dramatic—the resurrection of all the dead human beings.

Jesus Christ said, "Do not marvel at this; for the hour is coming in which all who are in the graves will hear His voice and come forth . . ." (John 5:28, 29). At His second coming, "many of those who sleep in the dust of the earth shall awake . . ." (Daniel 12:2). "For the trumpet will sound, and the dead will be raised incorruptible, and we shall be changed" (1 Corinthians 15:52). Therefore, if God has the supernatural turbo-power to resurrect dead human beings at the return of Jesus Christ, then surely He has the ability to bring back to life a mini-dog named Jax in His new earth if He so chooses. It would be as easy as snapping His fingers.

During my pet search, a gentle voice behind my mind seemed to whisper, "Read Romans 8." I had read this chapter before, but now something beckoned toward a closer look. After paging my way to this New Testament section, this is what I found:

> For the earnest expectation of the creature eagerly waiteth for the manifestation of the sons of God. For the creature was made subject to vanity, not willingly, but by reason of him who hath subjected the same in hope. Because the creature itself also shall be delivered from the bondage of corruption into the glorious liberty of the children of God. For we know that the whole creation groaneth and travaileth in pain together until now. And not only they, but ourselves also, which have the firstfruits of the Spirit, even we ourselves groan within ourselves, waiting for the adoption . . . the redemption of our body. (Romans 8:19–23, KJV)

These words deserve careful consideration. In fact, this has become one of my main there-might-be-hope-for-Jax sections. In my Bible prophecy seminars, I always encourage my audiences to put away preconceived opinions and to play close attention to the text— to the actual words of God. Only then can we really understand the message of truth. If we look closely at Romans 8:19–23, the concepts are truly amazing.

Paul revealed how Adam's sin effected the "whole creation" (v. 22), which must include the animals, too. Yet sin will not continue forever. In the interim, the "creature itself" (v. 21) is portrayed as "eagerly waiting" (v. 19), in "hope" (v. 20), while yet "groaning . . . in pain" (v. 22) until the full restoration after the second coming of Jesus Christ. Then "the creature itself also shall be delivered from the bondage of corruption into the glorious liberty of the children of God" (v. 21).

Did you catch that? After the return of Jesus Christ even "the creature itself *also* shall be *delivered*" (v. 21, italics added). To me, the words "also . . . delivered" seem to reveal the positive transition of Planet Earth and at least some of it's creatures from one state to another. The first state is one of bondage, corruption, and pain as a result of Adam's sin. The second state—after the second coming of Jesus Christ—is one in which "the creature [creation] itself" will also be delivered from this very corruption in order to share in the "glorious liberty of the children of God." It seems to me that Romans 8:19–23 implies that at least some of the creatures in this sinful world will be delivered from their present suffering resulting from man's sin and transported into the new earth.

That's a pretty powerful passage, isn't it? But guess what? There's an even better Bible section that gives me hope for Jax. In fact, if it wasn't for the discovery of this super-unique Bible passage, this book might not have been written. As we examine these verses, you be the judge. They're definitely about animals, their deaths, and their return to the dust. But then—at least it seems this way to me—they also talk about how God will bring them back to life again!

Of all the creatures God made at the Creation, there is none more excellent or so much to be respected, as a horse.

—BEDOUIN LEGEND

These amazing verses are found in Psalm 104. It's a Psalm of God's works, of His creation, and of His wonderful care for both man and animals. Written by King David, Psalm 104 mentions every beast of the field and the wild donkeys (v. 11), the birds (v. 12), the cattle (v. 14), the wild goats (v. 18), rock badgers (v. 18), living things both small and great (v. 25), the young lions (v. 21) and finally, man (v. 23). Ecstatic about God's creativity and His tender care for all His creatures, David burst forth with joy, "O Lord, how manifold are Your works! In wisdom You have made them all. The earth is full of Your possessions" (v. 24).

Read the following words very carefully:

> These all wait for You, That You may give them their food in due season. What You give them they gather in; You open your hand, they are filled with good. You hide your face, they are troubled; You take away their breath, they die and return to their dust. *You send forth Your Spirit, they are created*; And You renew the face of the earth. May the glory of the Lord endure forever; May the Lord rejoice in His works (vv. 27–31, italics added).

With a sense of awe I read that section again and again. *Wow!* was my exact thought. In the spirit of honest inquiry and with a true desire to accurately discover what the really Bible says, I will list five points worth considering:

1) Psalm 104 definitely concerns both man and animals.

2) The death of animals is described: "You take away their breath, they die, and return to their dust" (v. 29).

3) Then David seems to describe God bringing back to life at least some of the very ones that have died: "You send forth Your Spirit, they are created" (v. 30). Again, "*they* die . . . *they* are created" (Italics added).

4) This passage seems to point forward to the time of the new earth, for David continues, ". . . they are created, and You *renew* the face of the earth." This renewal also seems to parallel a New Testament prediction about how, after the second coming of Jesus Christ, there will come "the times of restoration of all things, which God has spoken by the mouth of all His holy prophets since the world began" (Acts 3:20, 21).

5) Finally, Psalm 104:31 looks into eternity with the triumphant shout, "May the glory of the Lord endure forever; May the Lord rejoice in His works."

After reading verse 31, I thought to myself, *Wasn't Jax one of God's works? Didn't the Lord create him and keep his little doggie heart beating for three happy years? And what about all those endearing and funny qualities that touched our hearts—wasn't God Himself the author of every positive personality trait?*

Of course, when God finally does create a new earth during "the times of restoration of all things," He surely has the option of making another dog comparable to Jax, or no dogs at all for that matter. But then again, why not restore to life that same little five-pound ball of fur? It makes sense to me that He might do this. Psalm 104 does say, "they die . . . they are created, and You renew the face of the earth" (v. 31). The bottom line is, whatever God ultimately decides, Psalm 104 gives me another reason to hope in *the possibility* that I might see Jax again.

Then another thought popped into my head, *What about God's promise to answer our prayers?* The Lord says, "Call to Me, and I will answer you" (Jeremiah 33:3). People often ask God for things and then watch Him "answer." Sometimes we pray for major things like forgiveness for some sin, for victory over powerful temptations, for guidance in choosing a marriage partner, for relatives who don't know His love, etc., etc. We also pray for smaller, more personal things like passing a school exam, for a virus-infected computer to start functioning again, for weight-loss assistance, for help in finding lost car keys, etc., etc. A real Christian is a praying Christian, and real Christians often thank God for large as well as tiny answers to prayer.

As I was studying the Word, and grieving over Jax, I thought to myself, *God has answered so many of my prayers, so what's wrong with asking Him to bring Jax back to life someday?* Jesus even said, "If you then, being evil, know how to give good gifts to your children, how much more will your Father who is in heaven give good things to those who ask Him!" (Matthew 7:11). Then I pondered, *Wouldn't seeing Jax again be a good thing?* It seemed so. Again I thought, *If I had infinite power, wouldn't I give this good gift to my child?* So shortly thereafter, Kristin and I knelt down in our sunroom and prayed a special, focused prayer to our loving heavenly Father in the name of His Son, Jesus Christ. I don't remember exactly what we said, but it was something like,

> Dear God, we really loved Jax, and we know You loved him, too. After all, he was one of Your works. The Bible says You do answer prayer, and so we ask You this specifically: When You finally do

remake the heavens and the earth, if it's Your will, please bring Jax back to life so we can see him again. In Jesus' name we pray, Amen.

I'm sure the good Lord heard that prayer, and so did His angels. It's a fact—a formal prayer from two sincere believers about a dog named Jax was lodged that day before the throne of the King of the universe. We trust our Father's heart. Ultimately, it's up to Him. We really hope He chooses to answer our humble request.

At the beginning of this book I listed some stories about how animals have rescued lost children or adults who had fallen into danger. Some of these tales are intensely dramatic, even worth reporting on CNN. Do you think God Himself might be involved behind the scenes in some of these stories? I do. In fact, the Bible itself records how God sent a bird to feed the prophet Elijah so he wouldn't die in the desert (1 Kings 17:4). Yes, God sometimes does mobilize His non-human creatures to help or save people in need, and I imagine that some of these rescue operations come as a direct answer to the prayers of humans.

In this light, is it so unthinkable that God might answer the prayer of a human by recreating a much-loved pet in the new earth, simply because we ask Him to? Concerning the resurrection of Jesus Christ, Paul said, "Why should it be thought a thing incredible with

> To the dolphin alone, nature has given that which the best philosophers seek: Friendship for no advantage. Though it has no need of help from any man, it is a genial friend to all and has helped mankind.
>
> —**PLUTARCH** (circa 45–125 A.D.)

you, that God should raise the dead?" (Acts 26:8, KJV). God is a miracle-worker. If He can resurrect the dead, then surely He can bring a tiny dog back to life. The Lord loves people and animals, and He definitely answers prayer. Will He answer our Jax-prayer? We hope so.

"For with God nothing will be impossible." Luke 1:37. God made Planet Earth in one literal week (Genesis 1 & 2). When He gave the Ten Commandments, He shook the ground of Mount Sinai (Exodus 19 & 20). Shortly thereafter, He opened the Red Sea for the Israelites to pass through (Exodus 14) and later caused the sun to stand still for Joshua (Joshua 10). In Babylon, He shut the mouths of hungry lions so they wouldn't eat his friend Daniel for supper (Daniel 5).

The greatest miracle of all occurred approximately 2000 years ago. The Eternal One even incarnated Himself into tiny microscopic cells inside the body of Mary (John 1:1–3,14; Matthew 1:23). Jesus Christ was born, grew up, lived, suffered, and died on a cruel cross to demonstrate God's love for man, and to atone for our sins. Then on the third day He rose from the dead (Matthew 28:5,6).

In view of such stupendous miracles, doesn't the Almighty have the power to re-create a mini-dog named Jax if He wants to?

I think so.

10

Mysteries of Heaven's Lamb

Man, do not pride yourself on superiority to animals; they are without sin, and you, with your greatness, defile the earth by your appearance on it, and leave the traces of your foulness after you—alas, it is true of almost every one of us!
Fyodor Dostoyevsky (1821–1881)

One of the themes of this book is that God not only loves people, but animals, too. After all, He created their beating hearts, intricate brains, breathing lungs, and functioning livers—plus their mysterious and almost human-like ability to suffer, cry, and even love. Yet for many animal lovers who read the Bible, a difficult question arises: If God cares so much for all His creatures, then why did He command Adam, Abel, Noah, Moses, King David, and millions of Jews to slice the throats of friendly lambs?

In order to understand this painful and repulsive practice, we must again go back to the book of Genesis. The Holy Book begins with this simple and majestic sentence: "In the beginning God created the heavens and the earth" (Genesis 1:1). On the first day He made the light (v. 3). On the second day He spread out the blue sky (v. 8). On the third day He formed Planet Earth itself with its peacefully rolling sea (v. 13). On the fourth day He made the brilliant sun, the reflecting moon, and all the shining stars (v. 16). On day five He spoke the colorful birds and numerous sea creatures into existence (v. 20). Then on the sixth day . . . Presto! . . . He formed the animals and then man (vv. 25 and 26).

"Then God said, 'Let us make man in Our image, according to Our likeness . . .'" (1:26). How marvelous! We didn't evolve from slime, goop, sludge, quadrupeds, mollusks, fish, or apes. Definitely not! The Bible says an all-powerful Creator—a God of love—originally made human beings in His own likeness. Thus the first man began with two legs, not four. His name was Adam, and his wife was called Eve. Then God placed our first parents in a beautiful garden called Eden.

Eden was a happy place, graced with crystal clear rivers, colorful flowers, magnificent trees, smog-free air, and yes, lots of furry, four-legged, friendly animals. Yet in the very midst of this perfect paradise grew a forbidden tree, "the tree of the knowledge of good and evil" (2:17). The Bible reveals that in His infinite wisdom, God made this tree to test the love and loyalty of Adam and Eve for their Maker. Did they appreciate the gift of life from the Almighty Giver? Were they thankful to have each other as companions? Did they appreciate even the furry animals He created to add to their happiness and enjoyment? Love for their all-gracious Maker, this was the core issue.

"The Lord God commanded the man, saying, 'You are free to eat from every tree of the garden. But you shall not eat of the tree of the knowledge of good and evil. For in the day you eat of it, you will surely die'" (2:16, 17). There it is, God's test of love, and His awesome warning of death if they purposefully chose to disobey. Amazingly, Adam and Eve failed the test! A highly-intelligent, super-tricky enemy seduced them from their loyalty (see 3:1–6). Eve "took of its fruit and ate. She also gave to her husband with her, and he ate" (3:6). This infamous act of ingratitude and rebellion against the expressed will of their Maker was not only wrong, but deadly. In the Bible, that act is given this name: Sin. Sin is *serious*.

"Through one man sin entered the world, and death through sin" (Romans 5:12). You may have a hard time believing this, but all of Earth's present problems, including the horrors of the Nazi Holocaust, the nightmare of starvation in Africa, the evil of child-abuse, the intense pain of September 11, 2001, and even the comparatively insignificant death of a small rat terrier named Jax—these are all ultimately rooted in that one bitter bite of forbidden fruit.

So what was a loving God to do? Should He allow Adam and Eve to perish in their sins, or implement a plan for their salvation? Fortunately for us, God chose the latter. Because death was the divine penalty for sin, His special plan out of necessity also involved death, even the death of His Son. That's why the Bible not only says, "The wages of sin is death" but also, "the gift of God is eternal life in Christ Jesus our Lord" (6:23).

Here's a very important question. How did God decide to powerfully illustrate His unique plan for our salvation? The answer is: *Through the death of His animals!*

Try to imagine this scene. A humble Jewish family has a little lamb that their children named Softy. He's so cute; they treat him like a pet. The kids love him, feed him, and sometimes even sleep with him. Yet one day their dad takes Softy away.

"Where's our little lamb?" the children ask their mom.

"Your father took him to the Temple."

"Oh . . . well . . . when are they coming back?" the kids ask nervously.

A tear forms in mom's eyes, she holds the boys close and whispers, "Boys, Softy is not coming back . . ."

Leading Softy with a rope, the father arrives at the Temple, and slowly approaches the altar of sacrifice. Softy isn't afraid, for he trusts his owner. After gently positioning the timid creature in front of him, dad places his quivering hand on the animal's unsuspecting head, much like a man would stroke his pet. He confesses his sins over it, representing the transfer of those sins to the innocent victim. A specially-robed priest then hands the father a razor-sharp knife, which he quietly slips under its woolly throat. The lamb tenses slightly, and swallows. Beads of sweat form on the man's head as his heart races wildly. Finally, the man closes his eyes and says a prayer. "Baa," says the lamb. In the next instant there is a horrific groan as the knife is plunged into the animal's warm flesh, and as its blood spurts and pours. Softy's eyes roll upward in that moment of shock and terror, and it's over.

In this awful ceremony—repeated millions of times in Jewish history—God was teaching the human race both the Bad News and the Good News. The Bad News is that sin is more serious than we realize, and its penalty is death. But the Good News is that our loving Creator decided to come to earth as a man and to offer His own life as a perfect sacrifice in our place.

All we like sheep have gone astray; We have turned, every one, to his own way; And the Lord has laid on Him the sin of us all.

—ISAIAH 53:6

The ancient Jewish prophets predicted that the Savior would come. Micah said His birthplace would be in Bethlehem (Micah

68

5:2). Isaiah said He would be like "a lamb led to the slaughter" (Isaiah 53:7). When Jesus Christ finally appeared on earth after thousand years of sin, sorrow, and animal sacrifices, a prophet named John shouted loudly, "Behold! The Lamb of God who takes away the sin of the world!" (John 1:29). The perfect sacrificial lamb had come in the person of Jesus Christ.

After Jax died, in the midst of my animal research, I was increasingly struck by the definite Jesus-animal connection revealed in the prophecies and described in the New Testament. In fact, the very last book of the Bible refers many times to Jesus as the Lamb (see Revelation 5:6,12; 6:1; 7:17; 13:8; 14:1,10; 15:3; 17:14; 19:9; 21:21; 22:1). Thus the Bible not only uses an animal to represent Jesus Christ, but this is also the primary symbol for Him in the book of Revelation.

Why a lamb? I pondered. *Why illustrate Christ's sacrifice by the death of an innocent creature?* Suddenly the answer burst upon me like sunlight from behind a cloud. From the very beginning in Eden, God must have created human beings and the more intelligent animals with a certain capacity to lovingly bond with each other. Remember, one of the very first things God did after He made Adam was to surround him with animals so he could name them. Thus the animals were originally created to be man's companions and friends. In other words, God designed human hearts and animal hearts to mysteriously connect.

After Adam and Eve foolishly fell away from their Creator, the Lord wanted to reveal to the whole human race the seriousness of sin, His plan of salvation, His desire to win our hearts. So what was the best way He could think of to accomplish these goals? The

69

incredible answer is: By telling human beings to take the very animals they were naturally designed to love, and to kill them!

It was hard enough to watch Jax get hit by a car and to see him bleeding in the street. But what if God told me to take a knife myself and slit his throat? I could hardly do it. It would be extremely difficult and painful. Almost impossible. *But that's the point.* By telling man to take an innocent, woolly, friendly animal—a lamb—and then to kill it with his own bare hands, this was God's way of trying to show us how horrible sin is and how awesome is the infinite sacrifice of Jesus Christ. "Kill the lamb," God commanded, "and realize it represents my Son who will die in your place for your sins." Such a painful, high-impact revelation should melt our hearts with His love and also lead us to turn away from our sins!

Paul wrote, "For I delivered to you first of all that which I also received: that Christ died for our sins according to the Scriptures, and that He was buried, and that He rose again the third day according to the Scriptures" (1 Corinthians 15:3,4). This is the Good News in a nutshell. Jesus is our sin-bearer, our all-sufficient sacrifice—*the final sacrifice* (Hebrews 10:12).

Have you ever had to euthanize your favorite dog, cat, bird, monkey, sheep, goat, or horse? A close friend of mine who is married and has two small children put his only dog to sleep recently. "It was one of the hardest things I ever did!" he moaned. In a sense, that's exactly what the heavenly Father did to

We can easily forgive a child who is afraid of the dark. The real tragedy of life is when men are afraid of the light.

—**PLATO** (427–347 B.C.)

His Son on the cross two thousand years ago. But Jesus Christ had to die so we could live.

> For God so loved the world that He gave His only begotten Son, that whoever believes in Him should not perish but have everlasting life.
>
> **—JOHN 3:16**

How should we respond to such love? The Bible clearly says we should:

1) "Repent," which means to confess and forsake our sins (Proverbs 28:13; Luke 13:3,5; Acts 2:38; 1 John 1:9).
2) Believe in Jesus Christ as our Savior instead of relying on our own goodness, works, or merits for eternal salvation (John 3:16; Ephesians 2:8,9).
3) Trust fully in God's grace and free forgiveness for every sin (1 John 1:9; Romans 4:7,8).
4) Receive by faith the power of His Holy Spirit into our hearts (Acts 1:8; Romans 5:5).
5) Because we love Him, live moral lives by the grace of God in harmony with the Ten Commandments (John 14:15; Titus 2:11,12; Revelation 12:17; 14:12).
6) Wait patiently for the second coming of Jesus Christ (Matthew 24:30,31,44; Titus 2:13; Revelation 14:14–16).
7) Look forward to God's new earth (2 Peter 3:13; Revelation 21:1–5).

After Jax died I read God's book, the Bible. The truth became so clear to me. I understood His desire for us to love His animals. I also knew why He said, "The lambs must die!" Then I saw *the Lamb*, and our loving God's perfect plan to win our hearts.

Twenty-three years ago I gave my heart to God. It was the best decision I've ever made.

11
Dead Dogs Don't Bark

A lie can travel halfway around the world
while the truth is putting on its shoes.
Mark Twain (1835–1910)

One of the most fantastic truths in God's book is the reality of the resurrection of the slain Lamb, Jesus Christ. 2,000 years ago our sinless Savior suffered intensely before He breathed His last breath on Calvary's cross; yet during the wee hours of the very next Sunday morning, the Lamb-Man literally burst forth alive from a cold and clammy grave (see Matthew 28:1–6).

Approximately forty-five years later—around 96 A.D.—in an extremely rare and unscheduled personal appearance, the Risen One revealed Himself to His friend John who, because of his faith, had been banished to a lonely Roman prison island in the Aegean sea. With "eyes like a flame of fire," the Exalted One declared, "I am He who lives, and was dead, and behold, I am alive forever more. Amen" (Revelation 1:14,18). According to the Bible, Jesus Christ has risen! and He is alive in heaven today, even though we can't see Him (1 Peter 1:8).

So what does the fact that Jesus lives and that He later made a personal appearance to John on the island of Patmos in 96 A.D.

have to do with our life in the twenty-first century? And what does it have to do with our animals? Simply this: Because people today love their pets so much, and because the death of an animal companion can be so incredibly painful, many grieving pet-owners are not only wondering if Spot lives today in heaven, but some are even pondering whether Rover or Snow Ball can possibly communicate with them from the other side.

In my Jax-research I was surprised to discover numerous accounts of individuals who claim that the spirit of their dead pet actually appeared to them from beyond the grave. Because of this growing trend, I decided to address this topic.

The Pets that Returned[6]

"Mr. Gerald Mills lives in the Northern town of Sheffield, Yorkshire UK. He has owned many pets during his lifetime but two have been extra special. This is his extraordinary story:

"Some years ago I was working in a factory in Sheffield when I noticed a little black kitten that was lost and on its own. The poor thing was covered in dirt and oil from the factory floor where it had been living. In truth I thought it would not live long as it was so weak when I found it. But I took it home and gave it some warm milk and a tiny bit of fish I had in the fridge. Then I placed it in an old shoe box with some clean dusters to keep it warm. The next morning the little kitten was still alive and looking at me as though I were its best friend. Well I suppose I was in a way. So I fed it some more milk and the cat purred so softly. I was really taken with it and gave it a name. I called the cat, Tiger, because it had stripes and was obviously a brave kitten.

"I already owned a dog called Suzy and soon Tiger and she were real pals. It was fun to watch them playing together. They were like that for many years, Tiger and Suzy side by side sitting in front of our coal fire, best of friends.

"Years passed by so swiftly, it hardly seemed any time at all since I first found that kitten. Tiger and Suzy had grown old together and now, as God would have it, they both became ill at the same time. I tried to nurse them, but it was time and rather than see them suffering I took both Tiger and Suzy to the veterinary surgeon. I held them in my arms as he helped them to pass over into the spirit world.

"It was some two years later that I noticed something strange at the foot of my bed. I was almost asleep when I first felt it, a kind of snuggly thing pressing against my feet. Immediately I thought of Tiger, she would often fall asleep on my bed and snuggle up near the foot of my bed. Looking down towards where I felt the pressure on my feet I saw, to my amazement, a cat. It was the spirit of Tiger come back from beyond to comfort me.

"As I stared in wonder at the 'ghost' of Tiger I heard a strange but familiar sound coming from downstairs. It sounded just like the barking of a dog. As I listened I recognized the bark as being that of my old friend Suzy. She too had returned to wish me well and let me know that in the future, when it is my turn to walk forward into the world of spirit, my pets will be there to welcome me. They were together still, Suzy and Tiger, alive and well in their spirit bodies."[7]

This is not an isolated incident. John G. Sutton is the author of the book, *Psychic Pets: Supernatural True Stories of Paranormal Animals*. One of the chapters in John's book entitled, *Gypsy the*

Singing Cat, contains a non-fiction account of "a cat voice" that supposedly sang "from beyond the grave."[8] I also came across another popular book called, *Ghost Dogs of the South,*[9] which has this summary statement on its publishers' web site advertising its contents:

> Digging deeply through the rich field of Southern folklore, the authors have discovered that a dog's devotion to its human does not always end at the grave. Dogs can be as peculiar as people. Their relationship with humans is complex. In story after story from Southern homes, there is strong evidence that this relationship can extend beyond death. Do dogs return from the other side to comfort and aid their human companions? You bet your buried bones they do.[10]

I'm sure you're aware that there are lots of so-called spiritualists, mediums, and psychics out there who claim the ability to communicate with the dead. But did you know that some of these profess an ability to contact not only those who had two legs, but also those with four? And with the increasing popularity of books like New York Times bestseller *Talking to Heaven: A Medium's Message of Life after Death,*[11] New Age radio programs like *The Next Dimension*, and psychic TV shows like *Crossing Over with John Edward* and *The Pet Psychic*, it seems the temptation is growing for more and more pet-grieving seekers to try and contact Fuzzy or Fido again.

In my research I also located the web site of Carla Person, a woman who features herself as a "Shamanic Healer and Animal Communicator," and one who definitely claims the psychic ability to contact our dead pets. On her internet home page I found this listed as one of the services she offers her many clients: "Learn how your special friend is doing in the afterlife, if/when she will return, and what messages she has for you."[12]

> Here's something to think about: How come you never see a headline like "Psychic Wins Lottery"?
>
> —**JAY LENO** (b. 1950)

Whenever a favorite animal dies, it's natural to wish it was still here. Kristin and I have been there and done that. This really, really hurts. But is it realistic to believe our dead pets are yet alive somewhere beyond our realm of time and space? In other words, have they now passed over into some spirit world? Can their ghosts still bark, baa, neigh, or purr? Do animals have separate souls that can exit their furry bodies, fly upwards to heaven, and then go back and forth between up there and down here, appearing or disappearing at will?

First of all, the Bible nowhere says that animals in this sinful world are by nature immortal, that they have separately conscious spirit-souls capable of leaving their bodies, or that these invisible, intelligent entities float upwards to heaven when they die. And there is definitely no "word from the Lord" in the Scriptures about any pet-ghosts making noises from beyond the grave. It's true, animals do have what the Bible calls "the breath of life" or "the breath of the spirit of life" (see Genesis 7:15,21,22; Psalm 104:29,30), but this breath or spirit is not an internally intelligent entity capable of exiting animal bodies, hovering over pet-graves, watching pet-funeral services, and later meowing in response to the beckonings of a spirit medium.

In fact, the Bible actually forbids all forms of attempted communication with those who have died, which, in principle, would certainly apply to God's lesser creatures. When the Israelites were about to enter the Land of Promise, the Lord strictly warned:

> When you come into the land which the Lord your God is giving you, you shall not learn to follow the abominations of those nations. There shall not be found among you anyone who makes his son or daughter pass through the fire, or one who practices witchcraft, or a soothsayer, or one who interprets omens, or a sorcerer, or one who conjures spells, or a medium, or a spiritist, *or one who calls up the dead.* For all who do these things are an abomination to the Lord, and because of these abominations the Lord your God drives them out from before you. You shall be blameless before the Lord your God. (Deuteronomy 18:9–13, italics added)

I realize these are strong words, but God knows they are needed. The reason for this counsel is because the Lord desires to protect His children, not just from the deception of phony psychics, but also from contact with real spirits. These may seem friendly, but their hidden agenda is not our happiness. Remember the super-tricky, highly-intelligent, invisible enemy who seduced Adam and Eve into sin? (see Genesis 3:1–6). Well, he still exists, and so do his angels. The Bible refers to this sinister being as "that serpent of old, called the Devil and Satan, who deceives the whole world; he was cast out into the earth, and his angels were cast out with him" (Revelation 12:9).

> In an age of universal deceit, telling the truth is a revolutionary act.
>
> **—GEORGE ORWELL**
> (1903–1950)

God's Holy Book has much to say about mediums and familiar spirits (Leviticus 20:6), and it's not positive. These things are placed in the same category as witchcraft (2 Kings 21:6). Biblically speaking, a familiar spirit is a spirit or ghost from the other side that looks, acts, and talks in a familiar way. These spirits usually take the form of dead humans, like one's cousin Ralph, or aunt Suzie. Based on books like *Psychic Pets, Ghost Dogs from the South,* and the spiritualistic activities of people like Carla Person, it seems they can even look like Fido.

But honestly, "familiarity" is not reality. Based on God's Word, we can safely say they are clever impersonations. These friendly-looking spirits are really dangerous fallen angels in league with Lucifer. The book of Revelation lifts the veil on these beings, saying, "They are the spirits of devils, working miracles" (Revelation 16:14). Therefore, just like the Titanic should have steered clear of the iceberg, even so should we steer clear of all mysterious beyond-the-grave human ghosts or pet spirits. On the other hand, we should know that real angels like the ones that spoke to Balaam, the virgin Mary, and Peter do sometimes appear in order to advance God's purpose (see Numbers 22:22–35; Luke 1:26–38; Acts 12:5–11).

Before I close this chapter, I want to clarify the basic biblical timeline so you can understand exactly when a person might hope to see a favorite pet again.

1. The Creation—God made a perfect garden in Eden for both human beings and animals (Genesis 1 and 2).
2. The Fall of Man—When Adam and Eve were seduced into sin by a beautiful, brilliant, fallen angel named Lucifer who used a serpent as his medium (Genesis 3; Isaiah 14:12–14; Ezekiel 28:14,15,17; Revelation 12:9). As a

result of sin, corruption and death entered our world, which also affected God's animals.

3. Fallen Human History—The zigzagging course of Planet Earth after sin entered (Genesis 6:5,11,12; Matthew 24:12-14). Animal sacrifices were initiated which pointed toward the future appearance and sacrificial death of the Lamb-Man, Jesus Christ (Genesis 3:21; 4:4).

4. The First Coming of Jesus Christ—The apex of God's awesome plan to save human beings from sin and death. On a cruel cross—Heaven's Ground Zero—the Lamb-Man died for the sins of the entire world (1 John 2:2). Jesus Christ was buried, rose again, and then ascended bodily to heaven (1 Corinthians 15:3, 4; Acts 1:9–11).

5. The Second Coming of Jesus Christ—The future climax of fallen human history. The Lamb-Man will return visibly at the end of this world (Matthew 24:14,27,30,31,44; 25:31,32; 28:20).

6. The Resurrection of Dead Humans—There will be a final, literal, bodily resurrection of both the saved and the lost (Daniel 12:2; John 5:28,29; Acts 24:15; 1 Thessalonians 4:16,17; Revelation 20:4–6).

7. The Final Judgment—When human beings are held accountable for their personal sins of breaking God's moral law and even for their cruel mistreatment of His animals. The lost will then realize why they are lost, that is, because they have persistently turned away from

> I tremble for my species when I reflect that God is just.
> **—THOMAS JEFFERSON**
> (1743–1826)

their Maker, His love, and from the fullness of Jesus Christ's sacrifice (Daniel 7:9,10; Ecclesiastes 12:13,14; John 3:16-21; Revelation 20:11–13).

8. Earth's Final Purification by Fire—In an awesome act of incredible majesty and infinite power, the Almighty will use high-temperature flames to completely cleanse Planet Earth from all the toxic effects of sin and Satan (2 Peter 3:7,10; Revelation 20:14,15).

9. The New Earth—After the final sanitizing of this sin-polluted earth and it's smog-infected atmosphere, God will wondrously remake the heavens and the earth to restore life as it was in the beginning (2 Peter 3:10–13; Revelation 20:15; 21:1).

10. The Creation of New Animals—In His new earth, the Lord God will once again create four-legged, friendly animals as loving companions for eternally saved human beings. But because sin will never occur again, these animals will never die (Isaiah 11:6,9; 65:17,25; Nahum 1:9).

I want to stress that it will be in the new earth that God will once again create His animals. And these kingdom-pets will not be floating spirits that soar down from heaven into perfect animal bodies. Not at all. If we stick with the Bible there's no real evidence that our dead pets are alive in heaven with Jesus Christ right now, and they certainly can't meow, bark, or woof at us from the other side. Thus the title of my book, *Will My Pet Go to Heaven?*, biblically, realistically, and sensibly applies to God's new earth, not to an immediate afterlife that may be entered at the moment of death.

As painful as it is for me and my wife, the fact is, Jax is dead and his tiny grave lies just west of Fort Worth. This is part of the reality of sin. The Scripture says, "All go to one place: all are from the dust, and all return to the dust" (Ecclesiastes 3:20). But the good news is, sin won't last forever and a new earth is coming. When heaven's clock finally ticks over to that time, there really is no biblical evidence that God will do anything other than what He did in the Garden of Eden, which was to form "every beast of the field . . . *out of the ground*" (Genesis 2:19, italics supplied). Therefore, just like in the past, God's future kingdom-creatures will come from the dust, not a spirit world. And it will be at this time that Kristin and I hope to see Jax again, if Jesus Christ so chooses.

Let hundreds like me perish, but let TRUTH prevail.

—MAHATMA GANDHI

(1869–1948)

No matter how popular the psychic radio programs and TV shows may be, I urge you to stay away from all mediums, paranormal psychic-communicators, and especially familiar spirits. If a ghostly apparition looks an awful lot like your grandpa Bill, your sister Martha, or even Snow Ball or Fido, don't interact with it; *it is a lie.*

I know the loss of any loved one is terribly hard. But really, the safest thing is to find solace in true earthly friends and in the living "God of all comfort" (2 Corinthians 1:3). Our heavenly Friend really cares, and He knows what it's like to lose a loved one. It happened to Him when His own Son died on a cross.

12
Pets, People, & Priorities

Of how much more value then is a man than a sheep?
Jesus Christ (Matthew 12:12)

God loves our pets, and He wants us to love them, too. But when it comes to intrinsic value, one human being—just one—is more precious to the heavenly Father than all the dogs that ever barked, all the cats that ever purred, all the birds that ever chirped, all the sheep that ever went "baa," and all the horses that ever neighed. Jesus Christ says to each of us, "*You* are of more value than many sparrows" (Matthew 10:31, italics added). In fact, if you could be placed on a shelf with a price tag, it would read, "Cost: The life of God's Son!"

When Kristin and I went through the pain of losing Jax, behind it all, this thought kept echoing in my soul, *If we care so much for a tiny terrier, how much more must God care for human beings?* Jax died less than two months after terrorist hijackers destroyed the World Trade Center and crashed into the Pentagon. Compared to the loss of husbands, wives, sons, daughters, and close friends who died at Ground Zero or on those American and United flights, our dog's death was nearly insignificant.

This "Human Beings Have Priority" issue is easily proven by once again taking a closer look at the original creation week. As we have already seen, during the first four days God created the light, the sky, the earth, the sea, the sun, the moon, and the stars. On the fifth day He made the birds and the fish. During the first part of the sixth day He formed the animals. After that, as His final act of super-creative genius, "The Lord said, 'Let Us make man in Our image, after Our likeness'" (Genesis 1:26). Thus man was made last, and he alone was formed in God's express image. In other words, God's crowning work had two legs, not four.

After Adam and Eve sinned, God's special plan was implemented for the specific purpose of saving humans, not animals. And as we saw earlier, throughout the Old Testament God was even willing to sacrifice animals to illustrate His plan. This fact alone should lead us to value people above pets. When Jesus Christ finally entered this world to offer His life as the ultimate sacrifice for sin, the Bible says, "Christ died *for us*" (Romans 5:8, italics added)—not for Fido, Fuzzy, or Black Beauty.

The more I think about the excruciating agony and infinite sacrifice of Jesus Christ to save human beings from sin and its attached penalty of eternal death, I must say that although I do appreciate the good deeds of the Humane Society, I value the work of the American Bible Society more. After His resurrection, Jesus didn't specifically tell His followers to "Go into all the world and rescue stray dogs," as important as this is. Instead He commissioned, "Go into all the world and preach the gospel" (Mark 16:15).

Therefore, our primary energies should be centered on reaching out to disoriented, mixed-up, lost human beings with the good news of the Savior who died for them. The fact is, our greatest happiness can never be found in an exclusive devotion to God's animals—even though sometimes they are easier to live with! Instead, it comes through discovering our Creator's love, in experiencing His awesome grace and forgiveness, and by a life of heartfelt service to other people created in His own image.

> Too often we underestimate the power of a touch, a smile, a kind word, a listening ear, an honest compliment, or the smallest act of caring, all of which have the potential to turn a life around.
> —**LEO BUSCAGLIA** (1924–1998)

It's awful to think about all the abandoned dogs that roam our streets without collars, yet a homeless child is worse. While it may be heart-sickening to imagine a crying puppy in the pound, how can this compare to the fading eyes of a starving boy or girl? While we may rejoice when a favorite cat hit by a Toyota recovers, what is this compared to the deliverance of a child-abused heroin addict from New York who surrenders his life to God's power? While God may smile when an Arabian horse's half-broken ankle heals, Jesus Christ taught that there is greater "joy in the presence of the angels of God over one sinner who repents" (Luke 15:10). In other words, when human beings repent down here, holy angels have a huge celebration up there!

Should we love the animals? yes. Be kind to God's creatures? of course. Enjoy their companionship? for sure. But let's never forget that the Creator of all life—in the form of a man—agonized, sweat drops of blood, wept, and died on a cruel cross for the specific purpose of bringing eternal life to human beings, not animals.

It's as simple as our ABC's. In the light of His infinite sacrifice, people come first, then pets.

Now, go do the right thing!
—DR. LAURA SCHLESSINGER

13

When Lions Don't Bite

Morning has broken
Like the first morning,
Blackbird has spoken
Like the first bird.
Praise for the singing!
Praise for the morning!
Praise for them, springing
Fresh from the Word!

Eleanor Farjeon (1881–1965)

In the Bible, there's a famous story about a man named Daniel who was thrown by his enemies into a den of man-eating lions. *He's toast for sure,* they thought. Yet after a pleasant night's sleep surrounded by furry "pillows," Daniel said, "My God sent His angel and shut the lions' mouths, so that they have not hurt me" (Daniel 6:22). The same God who had the power to make mean lions harmless has promised that some day every lion will be as tame as your kitty cat.

The book of Revelation records:

And I saw a new heaven and a new earth, for the first heaven and the first earth had passed away . . . And God shall wipe away every tear from there eyes; there shall be no more death, nor sorrow, nor crying. There shall be no more pain, for the former things have passed away. Then He who sat on the throne said, "Behold, I make all things new." And He said to me, "Write, for these words are true and faithful." And He said to me, "It is done! I am the Alpha and the Omega, the Beginning and the End. I will give of the fountain of the water of life freely to him who thirsts." (21:1,4–6)

A new earth is coming. It will be a Garden of Eden restored. God says so and His Word is true (v. 5). In that bright land all who have been redeemed through the shed blood and spotless righteousness of Heaven's Lamb will never die. Beyond this, there'll be lots of happy animals jumping around there. With beyond-this-world vision the ancient prophet Isaiah wrote:

The wolf also shall dwell with the lamb, The leopard shall lie down with the young goat, The calf and the young lion and the fatling together; And a little child shall lead them . . . They shall not hurt nor destroy in all My holy mountain, For the earth shall be full of the knowledge of the Lord, as the waters cover the sea. (Isaiah 11:6,9; 65:17,25)

How utterly fantastic! *Pets forever!* In that happy place there'll be no more people funerals, pet funerals, grief recovery groups, or need for Therapy Dogs International, Inc. to send its K–9 troops to a latter-day Ground Zero.

What will it be like to befriend a wolf, take a stroll with a leopard, ride piggyback on a gentle lion, or slide down the neck of a playful giraffe? Better yet, how would you like to be surrounded by a whole family of grizzly bears without

> Heaven is a city without a cemetery.
> **—AUTHOR UNKNOWN**

the slightest tinge of fear? Sounds like a dream, doesn't it? But it's true. God has promised, "These words are true and faithful" (Revelation 21:5).

A little girl from a smog-covered city went camping for the first time with her mother in the mountains. On their first night out, as the child stood outside their tent and looked up at the brilliant stars, she was amazed to see such beautiful dots instead of pollution and haze. "Oh mother," she reported excitedly, "If heaven is so beautiful on the wrong side, what must it be like on the right side!" How true! In this life we can only imagine the heavenly kingdom. But someday the haze will vanish and we will find ourselves in the midst of a perfect world with crystal clear lakes, smog-free air, gorgeous flowers, pleasant hills, happy humans, and super-dazzling beauty.

Kristin and I are really looking forward to being there. And of course we sincerely hope that one of our forever friends will be a tiny rat terrier named Jax whose fragile heart stopped beating on a dreary Halloween evening in 2001. When the good Lord finally recreates a pollution-free planet, and when His creative voice like thunder once again proclaims something like, "Let the earth bring forth the living creature according to its kind" (Genesis 1:24), we would love to see Jax reappear in a free-from-the-effects-of-sin immortal doggie body to dance, skip, prance, cuddle, and lick us once again. How wonderful this would be! Honestly, Kristin and I believe in *the real possibility* of this happening.

When it comes to the topic of our animals becoming kingdom-pets, I will now summarize the core concept of this book.

Our Creator is a highly personal and intensely loving God who originally formed His animals in the Garden of Eden to become friendly companions for human beings and to make them happy. In the galactic laboratory of His own eternal creativity, He not only designed human hearts to connect with each other and with Him, but He also added the extra blessing of fashioning human hearts and animal hearts in such a way that they would tenderly bond with each other.

As an integral part of this happy design, the good Lord specifically gave His more intelligent animals a certain capacity not only to think, but also to love. This special ability—the ability to love—most definitely sets the higher animals apart from the lesser creatures.

Even after sin, our wonderful God continues to love both people and their pets, and He is not unmindful of the affectionate and tender relationships established between them. If He numbers the very hairs on our heads (Matthew 10:30), then surely He also knows the number of furry strands on Fido!

The Lord is also the supreme and all-powerful One to whom "nothing shall be impossible" (Luke 1:37, KJV). In the light of the above concepts, which I consider to reflect solid biblical facts, it seems to me both reasonable and possible that in the new earth our loving God just might choose to snap His fingers, so to speak, and bring back to life certain animals that have become the special friends of His blood-bought children to enhance their eternal happiness.

For me personally, after Jax died, the thought that God might bring my beloved pet back to me in eternity helped relieve my suffering heart. As this idea dawned upon my wounded soul, I began to sense the comfort of His presence.

Nevertheless, I must go on record as stating clearly that even if that same little pooch is not recreated, this will not change Kristin or my love for God. We will still be satisfied, at peace, and happy. God's promise is: "And My people shall be satisfied with My goodness, says the Lord" (Jeremiah 31:14).

Above all—*wonder of wonders!*—Jesus Christ Himself will be there. With a tender heart He'll explain everything that has confused us on "this side of the river." As we look into His loving face and see the remaining nail-scars in His hands and feet, there'll surely be no disappointment. Along with millions of other human beings redeemed by His heart-ripping sacrifice, we will bask in His deep, untainted, infinite love forever. His love goes far beyond the love of any animal! Jesus proved His love on that dreary day so long ago on a hill outside Jerusalem when His own heart stopped beating.

Will my pet go to heaven? I sure hope so. Yet by far the bigger question is: Will you and I go to heaven along with our spouses, sons, daughters, parents, relatives, and those we love? As far as our beloved pets go, the issue for them is simply whether or not God chooses to recreate them in His new earth. But for us humans the far larger issue is whether we choose to repent of our sins, to trust fully in Jesus Christ and His sacrifice (symbolized by all those slaughtered lambs), and to follow the plain teachings of the Bible. If we do, then by His grace, we'll be ready for His soon return and will have a home in Eden restored.

Behold, I am coming quickly! Blessed is he who keeps the words of the prophecy of this book. . . . And the Spirit and the bride say, "Come!" And let him who hears say, "Come!" And let him who thirsts come. Whoever desires, let him take the water of life freely. (Revelation 22:7; 22:17)

Then the King will say to those on His right hand, "Come, you blessed of My Father, inherit the kingdom prepared for you from the foundation of the world." (Matthew 25:34)

As much as we love our animals, our own eternal life is more important than our pets. In the light of eternity, which is a very long, long, long time, it's a no-brainer, and making sure that we ourselves enter the "Land of No Good-byes" should be top priority. Bottom line: It's more important than Puppy Chow.

Kristin and I prayed really hard that Jax would live. When his glassy eyes finally faded into unseeing darkness, our aching hearts questioned, *Oh God, why?* Maybe this book is part of His answer. If our compassionate Creator can use my words to touch even one human life and lead that life to a better understanding of His tender love and purposes, then our precious Jax did not die in vain.

By the way, we finally did get another dog. He's a super-cute toy rat terrier who looks just like Jax! We named him Rerun.[13]

I hope to see you in God's eternal kingdom.

Endnotes

1. Taken from www.heinzdoghero.com—a *Heinz Pet Products* web site featuring their *Hero Dogs of the Year Awards: A Tribute to 47 Years of Amazing Canines*. For story details, click on *Timeline Of Heroes*.

2. *Newsweek: Special Report—After the Terror.* September 24, 2001. Article entitled, *The End of the End of History*, by Fareed Zakaria.

3. Taken from, *A Brief History*, found on TDI's web site explaining why their organization enlists animals to help humans. (see www.tdi-dog.org/abrief.htm)

4. Taken from the article, *Volunteers, The Spirit of America*, on TDI's web site (see www.tdi-dog.org/disaster.htm).

5. Also taken from the article, *Volunteers, The Spirit of America*, on TDI's web site (see www.tdi-dog.org/disaster.htm).

6. This story was taken from John G. Sutton, author of the book, *Psychic Pets: Supernatural True Stories of Paranormal Animals.* Beyond Words Publishing, Inc. (1998).

7. See www.pyschicworld.net/ppp.htm.

8. See www.pyschicnet.net/Psychic%20Pets.htm.

9. *Ghost Dogs of the South,* by Randy Russell and Janet Barnett. John F. Blair, Publisher (2001).

10. Taken from www.blairpub.com/folklore/ghostdogssouth.htm, the official web site of John F. Blair, Publisher.

11. *Talking to Heaven: A Medium's Message of Life After Death*, by James Van Praagh. Penguin Putnam Inc. 2001.

12. See www.spirithealer.com.

13. On pp. 51 and 52 of this book, all of the puppy pictures are of Rerun, as is the picture of the full-grown dog by the vent wagging his tail. All of the other photos are of Jax. Steve, Kristin, and Rerun are pictured on the back cover of this book.

To order additional copies of

Have your credit card ready and call:

1.800.795.7171

or send $9.95 each plus $4.50 S&H*

(*Add $1.00 S&H for each additional book ordered)

to

Texas Media Center

P. O. Box 330489

Fort Worth, TX 76163

www.petheaven.info

steve@petheaven.info

For more information about Steve Wohlberg's other books and tapes, or to receive his free newsletter, or to financially support his growing radio and television ministry, please contact:

Texas Media Center
PO Box 330489
Fort Worth, Texas 76163
Phone: 1.817.294.0053
www.endtimeinsights.com